ACADEMIC MANTRAS

ACADEMIC MANTRAS

Managing degrees of stress
during transitions,
crunch times, and
ego challenges

Joan R. Lerner, Ph.D.

LIFE EVENT PRESS　　　　　Philadelphia, PA

Copyright © 2013, 2015
2nd edition
Joan R. Lerner, Ph.D.
LIFE EVENT PRESS ▪ Philadelphia, PA

Library of Congress Control Number: 2013917685

Book design and typography by Ellen C. Dawson
Production by Julia Prymak/Pryme Design

Contents

Introduction   *vii*

SECTION I
Academic Transitions   *1*

MANTRA 1	■ School stress is in a class by itself	*3*
MANTRA 2	■ Positive or expected change is still stressful change	*7*
MANTRA 3	■ Anyone can be in awe of someone on campus	*16*
MANTRA 4	■ Exposure and intelligence are not the same entity	*21*
MANTRA 5	■ Past academic success predicts future academic success	*26*

SECTION II
Crunch Times   *31*

| MANTRA 6 | ■ Crunch time goes better with sleep, brief breaks, food, and water | *33* |
| MANTRA 7 | ■ Do something relevant every day to make progress | *38* |

MANTRA 8 ■ Productive procrastination is still procrastination   44
MANTRA 9 ■ Seek clarity for confusion ASAP   50
MANTRA 10 ■ Avoid doing something new or risky during crunch time   54

SECTION III
Ego Challenges   59

MANTRA 11 ■ Try not to rest your ego on one academic measure   61
MANTRA 12 ■ Educational success goes beyond grades and class rank   65
MANTRA 13 ■ Academic accidents happen   70
MANTRA 14 ■ Plan B may be better than Plan A   76
MANTRA 15 ■ Resumes express accomplishments   82

Index   87
Suggested readings   89

Introduction

I have been gathering information and professional experiences for this book for over 25 years, from the perspectives of working in counseling, teaching, and consultative roles, both in private practice and in university settings with educational groups from diverse disciplines.

The creation and format of this book was inspired by feedback from students and colleagues who were studying and working at highly regarded colleges and universities. Throughout my career I have heard educational concerns and helped decode stressful episodes which, upon cumulative observation and reflection, tended to occur most frequently at three key intervals: academic transitions, crunch times, and ego challenges. Along the way, I have received comments back both in real time and sometimes delivered years later, that one of my "favorite sayings" — which I now refer to as "Academic Mantras" — had been remembered and utilized as a lifeline during times of stress, such as encountering obstacles in completing a senior thesis or adjustments in returning to graduate school. Some of these individuals are now in mentoring positions themselves and have told me they incorporate said sayings in their own work with students.

One afternoon I was walking with my daughter, then an undergraduate student at the University of Pennsylvania, and had a chance encounter with a colleague, whom I had not seen in quite some time. My colleague enthusiastically told my daughter that he continues to reference one of my favored educational sayings in helping doctoral students to manage dissertation stress. My daughter smiled, hearing something that she had heard many times before, and agreed that she had found it very helpful in her own academic experiences as well. The format for this book had been put into motion!

This book is only possible because of the candor and insights of students and colleagues within the educational community, whom I have been privileged to get to know over the years. I am especially grateful for my experiences at the University of Pennsylvania, where I obtained my graduate education, worked in student counseling and as an instructor, and gained additional perspective as a Penn parent. The specific examples presented here have occurred repeatedly within the educational environment, under various circumstances, and were discretely chosen for their "human" quality. If you "recognize" yourself in any situation, consider that as validation that you were definitely not the only one in that position, but rather in good company.

This book is divided into three sections: academic transitions, crunch times, and ego challenges. Each section highlights five relevant Academic Mantras, with accompanying information to detail the concepts. As a whole, the fifteen Academic Mantras presented in this book are intended to help identify key issues, which can otherwise be felt but may go unnamed, thereby fueling uneasiness. Awareness is half the battle according to stress management experts. Included at the back of the book are references for key topics. This book is intentionally compact in deference to time constraints, and it is focused on material that can be applied to current and future situations, while providing perspective on past events.

My goals in writing this book are:

- to increase awareness of key academic pressure points, with the aim of improving prevention and preparedness
- to encourage swift and effective remediation when difficult situations arise

- to preserve self-esteem during ego challenges
- to promote future successes

These goals create the framework of this book and underscore the ongoing concern for encouraging the best possible educational experiences and outcomes in higher education.

■ ■ ■

On a professional note, I dedicate this book to students and their families and to educators, counselors, and mentors.

On a personal note, I dedicate this book to my parents who valued family and education most of all, to my husband and daughter for their love and support, and to my cousin, the "original" Dr. Lerner who led with excellence and integrity.

ACADEMIC MANTRAS

SECTION I
ACADEMIC TRANSITIONS

The starting or stopping of school is recognized as a major life transition by researchers and clinicians. Developmental psychologist Urie Bronfenbrenner, Ph.D. offered the perspective that development is optimized through the maximum of challenge and the maximum of support.

For most students entering a new competitive academic environment or, for that matter changing to the next semester, shifting activities, or preparing for graduation and beyond, the notion of challenge is virtually guaranteed, whereas the counterbalance of support is a possibility but not a given.

William Bridges, Ph.D., an expert on individual and organizational change, viewed the hallmark of transition as occurring in three segments: (1) an ending, followed by (2) a period of confusion, and (3) a new beginning. This sequence involves the notions of loss, uncertainty, and ultimate reestablishment over time. Students can expect this transition cycle to occur and recur at various intervals, underscoring the importance of support.

2 Academic Mantras

The five Academic Mantras in this section are presented to highlight the unique challenges that students face during academic transitions, and to offer assistance in helping students manage stress through awareness and action.

ACADEMIC TRANSITION MANTRAS

- ☐ School stress is in a class by itself
- ☐ Positive or expected change is still stressful change
- ☐ Anyone can be in awe of someone on campus
- ☐ Exposure and intelligence are not the same entity
- ☐ Past academic success predicts future academic success

MANTRA 1

School stress is in a class by itself

Higher education offers many tangible and intangible rewards, setting the groundwork for lifelong career development, strong friendships, and alumni ties. You will hear how fortunate you are to have this opportunity and that others would gladly take your place — and you know it's true — but the challenges of this endeavor cannot be minimized despite all of its advantages.

Those who had a rigorous high school experience may find that college presents additional challenges.

Those who had a rigorous college experience know that graduate study entails new dimensions. And if you stepped away from an exacting job, returning to school doesn't translate into *more* or *less* work but rather *different* work — there's no place like school. Where else can you sit in one room, surrounded by peers doing the same work, and be graded by the same standards, in the same time frame?

Each student will have their own viewpoint about the type of evaluation methods they face in their academic career and how stressful each measure seems to them. The rank ordering of "stressful measures," or potential "threats to competence," not only varies among student groups but can change over time within any individual, based on new experiences. Your own reactions to the variety of academic checkpoints such as taking tests, writing papers, making presentations, classroom participation in small or large venues, applied clinical work, research, interviews, and meetings with professors have implications for your time and stress management. Whenever possible, consider the mix of each semester's demands, such as test-driven or paper-driven classes and components of research or field work, when determining course selection, combination, and timing.

Academic pressures are unique. School is unlike any "real world" job where your success or failure typically does not hinge on how well you do in one particular snapshot of one key day. School in comparison has inevitable critical moments of standardized entrance exams, mid-terms and finals, and credentialing hurdles. In addition, feedback from some academic work may be spaced farther apart than feedback from your previous work or educational experience, leaving plenty of room between assessments to wonder how am I *really* doing. The mind abhors a vacuum and can fill that space with worry unless you self-monitor your thoughts.

The unique stress swirling in the academic environment is captured wryly by observer/writer Arthur Bloch, who addressed "academiology" in his *Complete Book of Murphy's Law,* highlighting the potential for ambiguity to increase with studying and the fear of being tested on missed information. These concerns are familiar and have been known to linger with students long after degree completion. At reunions, alumni, now seasoned professionals, can be heard relating that they continue to have "the school dream," in which requirements have not been met for their program, or that a registered class has not been attended or officially dropped. You may hear stories from family members, friends, and various campus sources about "memorable" tests, professors with difficult grading standards or curves, and students who have overslept and showed up late for exams. These events don't ever have to happen directly to you to feel the impact in the form of "second-hand academic stress."

All this may lead you, at times, to ask the question: Is this degree of stress worth it? Or as the MBAs ask: What about the ROI, Return On Investment?

The answer is still in process, and most who ask this question will, by the time of graduation and even more so looking back, solidly endorse their educational experience. A degree is not just measured in "dollars and sense," although educational attainment and higher income are positively correlated, though certainly not guaranteed. There is an academic mystique that follows outstanding educational institutions, and degrees become a short-handed way to telegraph an important accomplishment. Hopefully you will learn how to think clearly and how to address questions for a lifetime.

> Begin with the goal in mind — a valued goal — that comes with the best reassurance of all: A degree is yours forever!

MANTRA 2

Positive or expected change is still stressful change

Enrollment at a high-ranking undergraduate, graduate, or professional school is widely viewed as a positive, desirable life event that is met with congratulations. It is also a signal for an influx of rapid and multiple changes for students in terms of workload, identity, and lifestyle.

The amount of change, even if it is identified as positive in nature, can greatly impact one's stress level. The classic *Holmes and Rahe Stress Scale* measures the effect of life change events occurring for an individual within one year. The key premise is that life changes of various magnitudes include both *positive* life events, such as an "outstanding achievement," and *negative* life events, such as "change in health of a close family member." Various changes can be accommodated or may even stimulate productive action (eustress), but an overload of change can be a recipe for increased risk of impacting your immune system and susceptibility to illness (distress). Ultimately, stress management is a balancing act of change and stability, moderated by awareness, support, and actions.

Negative life event change is recognized as a time of upheaval and predictably elicits responsiveness from friends and family. If your parent is in the hospital, others may offer help by providing food or giving messages of support. In contrast, the need for understanding stress that is generated by certain positive life changes may not be readily apparent or may possibly be dismissed as not being a valid concern. Some of the most common and confusing scenarios for students have been expressed over the years, with the following variation on this theme:

> "I don't get it — I just started in the college/
> master's/doctoral program of my choice,
> moved into a great new place, found a
> convenient part-time job in my field, met

some interesting new people — what's wrong with me for feeling overwhelmed and complaining about good things happening? Isn't this what I *really* wanted?"

This reaction is better understood when reviewing the situation with the recognition that the amount of life change is significant, particularly if you look at the domino effect to include probable changes in academic and/or work schedule, sleeping and eating habits, financial state, residential relocation, and altered social activities. These changes add up to challenges of adjustment. Extra attention and ongoing decision-making is needed for forging career and personal pathways, as well as addressing routine matters such as: Where do I get my lunch? When do I have time to eat lunch, and with whom?

Individuals can differ in their assessments of change and in their reactions to a specific transition. For one person, a particular change such as moving to a new city may be a minor stressor due to prior life experience and personality. Another person who lived in one location their entire life or prefers more familiarity might find the identical move to a new city to be a major stressor with novel considerations. Ask yourself what is the real impact on you personally, and what can you do to make it easier, such as gaining local information, utilizing campus resources focused on adjustment and transition, and inserting some added routine into your schedule. Studying in a favorite spot, centering the week by a regular social or recreational activity, or writing in a journal may be helpful. Familiar or "transitional" objects from one's prior environment, including personal photos and school mementos, can serve as touchstones of continuity.

Change, even when positive and expected, involves a process of acclimation to a new environment that is not automatic, despite being physically on site. It takes time to feel at home in a community within the many groups of classroom, work, and living environments. In addition, as Bernice Neugarten, Ph.D., a developmental psychologist who coined the term the "social clock" noted, adults may feel "on time" or "off time" in relation to their pursuits and their peers, as adult development has far more variability than child developmental milestones. One can find oneself in the same year in college or starting graduate school with gap-year or multi-gap-year students, career changers with an entire professional life left behind, and classmates who are single, partnered, or have children.

At any point, longing for something from your pre-transition time or homesickness may occur. You may miss a particular person, miss the predictability of your prior routine, or just miss your former level of competence before the change, when you may have been in a more confident or established position. Graduate students who are returning to school after being in the work force note the transition from professional role to student status, which can vary in magnitude of changes based on prior responsibilities, length of time away from academics, and current life circumstances. Last year's seniors becoming this year's freshmen express their own concerns of beginning again and reestablishing themselves in a new environment.

Academic transitions occur not only as a onetime starting point, but cycle throughout the degree process in major and minor ways as schedules change on a quarterly, semester, or yearly basis, including:

- adjustment to enrollment and entry into the school;
- the start and stop of each semester;
- the introduction of field work, clinical work, and internships;
- major writing, thesis, or research paper endeavors;
- the fulfillment of academic requirements and preparation for graduation;
- applications for jobs or additional academic pursuits, together with their anticipated transitions.

Academic changes and transitions can be felt more intensely with the following personal scenarios or backdrops:

- feeling of being *on* or *off* time in terms of what you expected for yourself or in comparison to others' choices, such as which semester you're abroad/not abroad, or returning to school for advanced degrees at various timetables;
- being the first generation in your family to obtain a college degree or graduate education;
- being the first in your family to specifically become a physician, lawyer, educator, and so on, or the first person *not* to go into the family profession or business;
- initiating a change in major or specialty within your program and refocusing, with the consequence of possible lost time or needing to meet additional requirements;
- entering new phases of academic work such as clinical rotations, research, or major writing that taps into other skills that may be out of your comfort zone;
- revising academic time structure itself by creating the time management challenge of self-structuring, after having been accustomed to a relatively evenly paced schedule — from having set class hours, to being more remote

with dissertation or independent study, or simply having no classes on certain mornings, afternoons, or days.

Since these educational transitions are largely predictable in sequencing nature, you can take an active stance to make their arrival easier by front-loading certain activities whenever possible:

- physically plan ahead and settle in with needs of academic and household supplies, and fully unpacking or decorating your space if it's new;

- orient to the campus, school, or internship by attending welcome events and open houses, introductions to the library system, computer facilities, and university life offices for academic, career, or personal support;

- identify social resources including dining places, recreational facilities such as gyms, music practice rooms, lounges, and TVs;

- read the city newspaper, campus newspaper, or individual school's newsletter;

- get an academic heads-up of what courses you are considering: review relevant books in the school bookstore and syllabi from previous years, professor and class ratings, and professor publications;

14   Academic Mantras

- identify areas of personal concern that could use updating, such as computer knowledge, math review, writing and study skills, presentation skills, resume and interviewing skills. Utilize campus resources that can help you assess and address your needs from an objective perspective.

In addition to identifiable life events and changes discussed, there's one aspect of stress that often goes overlooked — the occurrence and impact of daily stressors. The *Hassles and Uplifts Scale,* devised by psychologists Richard S. Lazarus Ph.D. and Susan Folkman Ph.D., measures an ongoing tally of routine stresses that can serve to irritate (hassle) you or provide a perk (uplift). The accumulation of stressors in every day life, such as hunting for keys, reveals the power of ordinary repetitive occurrences to distress us, as well as to delight us, such as running into a friend. Remedy unnecessary *hassles* with added organization or back-up resources, and actively seek out *uplifts* to balance out the stress equation. Whatever you did for stress management prior to this transition — including personal interests, creative outlets, exercise, recreational and social activities — needs to be remembered, applied, and fit into this new environment.

> You are the constant in your own life and need to maintain ongoing self-awareness while assessing emerging demands and changes.

MANTRA 3

Anyone can be in awe of someone on campus

The competition for enrollment in particular institutions and programs tends to get steeper each year and more selective at every level. Top ranked programs attract excellent students, including a multitude of valedictorians and salutatorians, National Merit Scholars, advanced placement test-takers, and academic award winners. Graduate school students may have earned college degrees with honors, been awarded Phi Beta

Kappa keys, published research papers, participated in significant field experiences, and obtained high entrance and board scores.

Other talents also abound in the form of varied achievements. Your class may include accomplished musicians, actors and actresses, champion athletes, book authors, inventors, business creators, and more. This is in addition to the high percentage of individuals who distinguished themselves within their school environment by being the student class leaders, editors of the newspaper, and debate champions.

Sometimes the academic strengths of particular classmates will go under the radar until it's discovered that someone is enrolled in the most advanced math class, obtains a prestigious internship, or writes a commanding editorial in the newspaper. Even seemingly ordinary social moments can make an impression as you are walking to class behind someone who appears to know everyone on campus or notice your teaching assistant with his or her small child and wonder, "How do they manage it all?"

You may also meet classmates with famous family members who are well-known in the arts, business, educational, and political worlds. Additionally, classmates may be tied to intergenerational legacy or have a relative teaching at the same institution. Some students may never have stepped on the campus before, and others may have been there for prior academic work or to visit family and friends. Everyone brings a different set of experiences and their own talents to the same academic meeting spot.

Over the years I have seen high achieving students of all backgrounds privately worry about being "good enough," as they become aware of their own limitations in relation to the vastness of knowledge within their fields of study. At the same time, students may discount or overlook their own abilities, while noting the accomplishments of others. Student's reference points may be varied and numerous, and include peers within their own program, as well as family, friends, and acquaintances at other campuses. Often a student will identify someone else's particular educational or work achievement, outstanding talent, or life experience that is impressive to them, especially one that may be apart from their own skill set or background. Initially, students may be more focused outwardly and may not consider the reciprocal possibility that they too may impact peers with their own special merits.

The difficulty level of the academic work and tasks at hand are sometimes overlooked as topics for discussion. Across programs, certain students have a self-presentation style that give the appearance that they are consistently gliding through school, without any indication of possible concerns with varying endeavors. Yet underneath, unseen, significant effort may be taking place, with studying hard, and worrying at times to do well. This can make it difficult to gauge one's own efforts or to assess the full exertion of others focused on the same materials. Perhaps raising a general question or making a specific self-disclosure in a sub-group or on an individual basis could open up avenues for helpful perspective.

In addition to new peers, students are studying in an environment that involves the academic community at large. There are alumni with remarkable achievements and professors, renowned in their field, who literally have written *the* book on their topic. It may be someone's life work that ultimately inspires you towards future direction in your own career. The goal is to learn from the academic community and to have others learn from you too. It may turn out to be a student comment or unexpected question punctuating a lecture that spurs academic synergy or the next research idea.

Over time, familiarity with the environment and with others will tend to increase your academic comfort level, hopefully moderated by your own self-esteem, and support from others. Think about your self-development from the perspective of what you have accomplished over the years; the younger self might have been awed by where you are today. Update any gap in self-image. Nathaniel Branden, Ph.D., psychotherapist and author of *The Six Pillars of Self-Esteem,* underscores the notion that self-esteem relies on confidence in one's thinking and coping ability, and confidence in having rights and being worthy of obtaining one's goals. Try to avoid having separate standards for others and often impossibly harder standards for yourself. Counter any thoughts or actions of "self-discrimination" by asking yourself: What if this were someone else, a respected peer, and not me?

Address any discrepancies in your response.

After all, you are in the class.

> Each individual adds to the learning environment and to the academic community.

MANTRA 4

Exposure and intelligence are not the same entity

It is a daunting task to try to keep up with the immense amount of established information, changing information, and new information in any field regardless of strenuous effort and keen intelligence. One cannot have exposure to everything.

Case in point: During a talk on stress management and transitioning to graduate school, I asked participants if they knew the significance of a particular term. Some students smiled with amusement, and others seemed to be searching their memory for any recollection. In actuality, my question did not refer to some important person, obscure academic principle, or acronym but instead was linked to a children's television show. Graduate students who were parents or who had small children in their lives may have seen the program. One could not possibly have known the answer to the question unless there had been prior exposure to the TV characters — regardless of intellectual ability. The intended takeaway message was twofold: (1) exposure has its own key part in navigating the learning equation, and (2) no one can expect to know or be aware of everything — it's not humanly possible.

A new learning environment or different field may usher in the need to identify and familiarize yourself with additional reference points common to your current program and cohorts. This can include expanding your vocabulary, and seeking out key sources of information such as preferred professional journals, professors' research, national, international, and school newspapers, as well as after-hours meeting spots and social activities. It is important to fill in any missing information by asking questions when something is unfamiliar and to actively seek out new contexts to bridge exposure gaps. Doing so will help you be able to join in the conversation and to be more connected in the process.

Carol Dweck, Ph.D., psychology professor and motivation researcher, looks at the notion of how mindset affects learning. Dweck's research speaks to "fixed mindset" versus "expandable" or "growth mindset." Students with fixed mindsets are focused on being "smart" and may not move toward, or even avoid, areas where they don't "look" as smart. Whereas those with expandable or growth mindset are focused on increasing mastery and are less concerned with being "right or wrong." A key difference between these mindsets is in the interpretation of learning situations, and the focus on capacity for change and adjustment, by putting forth the effort required to address the challenge at hand. This notion of mindset is a powerful factor in educational experience, subsequent work, and lifelong learning.

Thanks to great technological advances, we expect access to information instantly, but learning itself takes time, repeated and prolonged exposure. Some students may experience varying degrees of frustration or discomfort if they do not readily grasp unfamiliar material, or if they have unanticipated difficulty with untangling the confusion. In these situations, there is a need to tolerate initially not knowing, or being confused, until one can progress through the learning cycle to accumulate additional understanding, and hence increase the feelings of competence — which may be challenged again at the next level of learning integration. Research by

Herbert A. Simon, Ph.D., a Nobel Prize winner in economics who studied decision-making and learning, suggests that to be really *expert* in a field there is a "10 year rule" of investing in intensive work and gaining a vast number of "chunks" of knowledge. Motivation is a key determinant in developing expertise, as it takes dedication to amass the experience and complex understanding over extended time.

Practically speaking, even with having an open mindset and great motivation, it is advisable to not overlook the role of course challenge in managing your workload. For instance, skipping over course levels or taking certain classes may require added time and effort to compensate for the lack of prior contact with specific academic materials. New learning is usually more time consuming and less predictable, and it may be helpful to balance novelty and continuity. Stylistically, some students report a preference for having information on what's ahead in the academic landscape and may learn better by gaining increased familiarity or having an overview in place before proceeding. Reading or reviewing basic or introductory material that is written in clearly defined language, without assuming prior knowledge, can provide an opportunity to fill in missing or weak background areas.

> Exposure and intelligence are separate entities that need to work together.

MANTRA 5

Past academic success predicts future academic success

By this point in your academic career, you may have taken countless numbers of tests and produced volumes of written material. There is a considerable academic "permanent record" associated with your name after all these years of schooling. Higher educational institutions are well-practiced in screening for successful candidates, and when offered admittance to a program there is every expectation that your future success is achievable based on your educational history.

The notion that past academic success predicts future academic success makes a great deal of intuitive sense. Of course, a positive outcome also requires that academic success is not taken for granted. There is a need to stay focused, utilize study skills, ask questions, seek assistance, and practice good self-care. Task demands often vary within the class or throughout the program, which necessitates monitoring the pace and at times increasing effort to meet a particular challenge.

When transitioning into a new academic situation, self-directed questions and personal doubts may emerge. Students in undergraduate, graduate, and professional school programs across disciplines may experience what psychologists Pauline Clance, Ph.D. and Suzanne Imes, Ph.D. coined as the "impostor phenomenon," based on findings in working with capable professionals who expressed feelings that didn't seem to "fit" their achievements. The impostor phenomenon is a fear that your prior success is attributable to "luck" or can be viewed as a "fluke," and that future success may not be repeated, and you may be found out to be a "fake." The *Impostor Phenomenon (IP) Scale* has applicability for academic populations, who focus on issues regarding testing and evaluation, have concerns about competence and capability, and worry about paths to achievement and sustainability of successful performance.

The good news — if you are feeling like an impostor in the group — it is not unusual. It is often reassuring for students to hear during orientation sessions how common the impostor phenomenon is, but often not discussed, and to find responses in any incoming class that indicate how many feel like they were admitted by luck or mistake. The evidence of your prior success has many reference points and cross-validations. You may be fortunate with an occasional test question or essay topic, but overall, time and again, course after course, case after case cannot realistically be discounted. The impostor phenomenon may be felt more intensely during next level transitions and challenges as well, such as thesis writing or clinical experience. Here is where a knowledgeable mentor, advisor, or counselor can help with perspective on how you are progressing in the field, especially when measures of how you are doing are rarely self-evident, or expressed as right/wrong absolutes.

Students also bring their "educational memories" dating back to childhood with them to the next academic phase and classroom experiences may be remembered at various points. Over the years I have heard students recounting about having had difficulty on a test, writing assignment, presentation, or stage performance and/or having received negative feedback from a teacher or classmate. Although these events may have happened in the distant past, occurred infrequently, and not had impact on an official record, they can leave traces of concern that such events may happen again and cause difficulty. Review the past academic incident to make it a contained circumstance, not an undercurrent, and consider the developmental aspect of the learning process; one may have become a better student over time. Greater experience can translate into greater savvy with addressing tasks and demands of the environment. Lessons learned can provide increased self-awareness in terms of interests and support for success — including learning style of visual, auditory, or kinesthetic preference, and how to utilize resources.

In addition to gaining clarification of any past concerns, benefit from focusing on all that went right and what went *particularly* right for you. It can be helpful when students are asked to relate their greatest accomplishments and be encouraged to remember these key successes. Important prior successes can serve as meaningful self-references and sources of motivation. Take your best experiences of achievement or where you overcame obstacles to succeed out of your comfort zone and create your own academic mantra of encouragement. Some examples:

- If I could get an A in Professor X's class, I can manage on this test.

- If I could speak in front of my entire class or at a conference, I can face other audiences.
- If I could write a major research paper, I can write a thesis.
- If I could pass my driver's test with both knees shaking, I can rise to the occasion as needed.

> Utilize your own mantra of accomplishment as a framework for success.

SECTION II
CRUNCH TIMES

No matter how well-organized you set out to be each semester, you will likely face the scramble for time during the highest demand periods of tests, papers, and activities that bunch together. Be ready for it — crunch time alert! Let friends and family know your crunch time schedule and that your availability may be limited by impending study needs.

Time pressures can generate "hurried sickness" — feeling rushed or too frantic to take full notice of what is occurring. Jon Kabat-Zinn, Ph.D., a mindfulness and stress expert, advocates being fully present in what you are doing to slow things down and concentrate. Students need to actively guard themselves from inner distractions of skipping over to worrying about the *future*, instead of worrying directly about the test or paper, and managing the noise from the outside environment.

The five Academic Mantras in this section are presented to highlight the relationship of crunch time and stress and to articulate the challenges of most effectively utilizing time and energy under pressure. It is a given that there will be too much work to do. Managing this feat requires your well-placed attention, understanding from others, and self-care.

CRUNCH TIME MANTRAS

- ☐ Crunch time goes better with sleep, brief breaks, food, and water
- ☐ Do something relevant every day to make progress
- ☐ Productive procrastination is still procrastination
- ☐ Seek clarity for confusion ASAP
- ☐ Avoid doing something new or risky during crunch time

MANTRA 6

Crunch time goes better with sleep, brief breaks, food, and water

The reason why I start crunch time mantras in this fashion is that the "basics" can be taken for granted and become jeopardized in demanding times, often triggering negative consequences. Recall the humanistic psychologist Abraham Maslow, Ph.D. and that the *Hierarchy of Needs* starts with the physiological requirements that must be met before other personal concerns and strivings can be achieved.

Yet even if you sense that this particular crunch time is more challenging than previous crunch times, or feel that you have made your own crunch time mess worse, you can't work well under conditions that wouldn't pass employment standards.

Sleep is often the first area sacrificed when time pressures mount. You may be able to adjust your usual sleep schedule — but only to the extent needed to remain functional. Variables, such as the specific pressures, and the number of nights affected by them, will determine the viability of this strategy.

In *Brain Rules,* developmental molecular biologist John Medina, Ph.D. discusses the importance of "sleep well, think well" and gives research evidence for how "sleeping on a problem" actually helps integrate material that the brain is actively trying to solve, and how sleep deprivation impacts both learning and well-being.

It can be useful to develop an internal gauge of your own sleep awareness and personal effectiveness. Some students have looked at solving the daily Sudoku or crossword puzzle in the newspaper as an "alertness measure" and reference point of when their attention might be lagging. Other students read chapters for one specific course or view comprehension in a particular lecture class as the reference point for deciding when sleep is needed over studying. When reasonably rested, you can process complex materials more quickly and make up the time. You may be misleading yourself by staying up *extra late* and just glossing over pages or by aiming to wake up *too early* for productive work and paradoxically losing time due to concentration issues or oversleeping.

Taking a brief break from studying can refresh your mind and improve your ability to identify solutions for how to proceed or reframe questions. Innovative companies and workplaces are championing this notion and incorporating a range of helpful options from exercise to designated quiet or nap spaces. Even if you are sitting at your desk, just thinking of a positive daydream can provide relief, as the mind responds *as if* something actually occurred; picturing yourself finishing a paper or test, or thinking of getting a desired job offer can be an uplifting thought. The idea is to actively put the work aside and have a reprieve from the task. Students can benefit from taking a break outside of academic work, separate from calculating grades with various test outcomes, or thinking about next semester's challenges and schedule.

Brief breaks are a necessity, not a luxury, although is may seem counterintuitive at times to pause when seeking progress. Please do not feel guilty taking a break, as this detracts from the purpose. Many students have reported that they don't ever feel the work is off their shoulders until the semester is actually over —

which is too long to wait for a break. There's always more to do, but you have to call it a night — close out a chapter or compartmentalize to pick back up and match the best time of day for concentration. Work/life balance at this time may be limited to key relationships and connecting mainly around meals, studying, or exercise, and you may lament or resent the lack of time for engaging in the fuller array of personal life activities. It can be helpful to make plans for after crunch time and have things to look forward to on the other side; positive anticipation is found to increase enjoyment by "saving" something good to enjoy at a later time, such as thinking about an upcoming vacation.

When it comes to eating as part of self-care, it can be understood that for many crunch time translates into added munch time. In his book *Calm Energy*, Robert Thayer, Ph.D. addresses how food is used during stressful times to try to self-regulate moods of tension and fatigue by seeking high calorie food choices. Healthy food needs to be added into the equation and perhaps meals can be reframed as an important break, taking a few minutes to literally and figuratively refuel. It may be more effective at times to actually sit down to eat, instead of choosing everything "to go." Being rushed doesn't necessarily translate into saving time, especially if you're multitasking and balancing food with high spillage potential. During days of longer study hours, consumption of caffeinated beverages, particularly coffee, tends to rise. Meanwhile, water intake/hydration needs to be remembered as well (check current health guidelines).

Crunch time, by definition, is time-limited and requires more focus and commitment to the task at hand. It is not a time to debate the larger questions of "Do I really want a double major, What specialty area might I pursue, or Why did I trade a paycheck for advanced training?" After crunch time you will have less time pressure and better perspective to review and reflect upon these activities and choices. Try to plan for some recovery time on the other side, as crunch time can put you through the "adaptation cycle" identified by stress expert Hans Selye, M.D., Ph.D., as "alarm–resistance–exhaustion." Perhaps you will emerge from crunch time with an even greater appreciation for work/life balance, including the return to studying at a more relaxed pace.

> First just get through crunch time as a goal in itself — hopefully made more bearable with a measure of self-care.

MANTRA 7

Do something relevant every day to make progress

Thinking and thinking and thinking about doing something, without taking any action, can utilize a great deal of energy and exhaust you before you even get started. Ask yourself: What have I actually worked on today? If you are spending more time worrying than taking steps to problem solve, study, write, or look for a job, recognize that you may need to refocus your efforts to make better progress.

Doing something realistic to advance your position, even a seemingly minor something, such as making an appointment to speak with a professor or reading a suggested paper, adds to a sense of efficacy and chips away at the task. Being active on a consistent basis helps you to coexist with the stress, feel more in control by taking positive action, and become desensitized enough to address materials; ignoring your work builds greater stress. If you find yourself unable to take such steps on your own, it is a signal to enlist the attention of a helpful other to jumpstart the process by providing support or identifying obstacles to get unstuck. Sometimes it is a classmate, professor, or counselor who can ask a question or offer an idea that can help you regain your momentum or identify the need for more ongoing assistance.

Significant tasks need to be fully operationalized into specific steps for completion. Concretes are less stressful than abstractions — particularly emotionally charged abstractions, such as elevating a thesis to a symbol of one's life education, as opposed to being a very important task or requirement that is serious but *real* and attainable. A "paper," even a BIG paper or thesis, is something that has to move from your mind as a concept to becoming definable to all: x number of pages, a table of contents, labeled chapters, a bibliography, and personalized with an introduction, acknowledgment, or dedication page. A "test," even a GIANT test, is comprised of *x* number of questions, regarding specific articles, assigned texts, and lecture notes. Thinking and applying to a "job" or "internship" will also need to be deconstructed into concrete components that can be acted upon. You can address tasks in various stages or parts, sequentially if needed, or in your own organizational order if possible.

In addition, to help make progress, there are key time management rules *in general* and your own *personal* rules to integrate into your schedule. Here are three key general rules to keep in mind:

PARKINSON'S LAW

Time expands to fit whatever time is allotted or available. Translation: if the paper is due at 5:00 p.m., you may be submitting close to that time, same day. This concept can be applied to the personal realm as well: If you don't have to be somewhere until 11:00 a.m. on the weekend, you may not be ready until minutes before, perhaps rushing at the end. Deadlines speed up the process and can set the pace. Some people are more or less sensitive to this issue depending on their sense of time and ability to self-structure, and they may benefit from inserting opportunity for accountability and meeting with others. This may be especially important during open-ended time periods such as reading days or thesis writing. Apportion your time and create your own divisions or deadlines.

PARETO PRINCIPLE OR 80/20 RULE

This rule involves the notion of disproportionate relationship between effort and reward. It implies that you will receive 80% of your benefits from 20% of your efforts. Find the key resources, information, and people to provide the most impact and satisfaction. During crunch time your may have to triage best yield materials, even if your preference would be to read everything thoroughly. Adjust your focus accordingly.

MURPHY'S GENERAL RULES

- Nothing is as easy as it seems
- Everything takes longer than you think
- Whatever can go wrong, will

The academic takeaway from Murphy is to start unknown or "variable" tasks earlier, such as paper writing and studying for tests in which it's harder to predict exactly how much time will be needed for completion, versus the more predictable time needed for typing the paper or taking the test. Consider budgeting more time than you initially think may be necessary to allow for flexibility in adapting to unexpected complications or mishaps. In comparison, "fixed" time tasks are more predictable in parameters and can be scheduled more closely, such as attending classes back to back. Note that *fixed* time has the potential to become *variable* time if time parameters are ignored or unexpected factors arise that need attention.

The personal time rules are about knowing yourself and your preferred work style. For instance, if you are sharpest in the morning, try to address your most complex work then, and shelve the morning newspaper until a later break. You may prefer to have larger chunks of time, but try to utilize small snatches of time for mundane organization, references, or errands along the way. If you work better with a friend in your space, plan accordingly. If you prefer quiet, music, slight background noise, home, library, or outside study spot, and for which tasks — pair consistently to optimize your study strategy. Be aware of the pitfalls of multitasking and study environments. Larry Rosen, Ph.D., an authority on learning and technology, has found that current environments are more distracting than some may recognize and recommends "turning off" technology for certain periods of study.

Good work habits can increase well-being and build the momentum to navigate the. "fight or flight" stress response; routinely facing your work allows you to address the stress (fight) and not react with avoidance behavior (flight). Additionally, it is useful to regularly note any loose ends that emerge with work demands, such as restocking supplies or arranging a group meeting. Be sure that your intention to do something has been executed and that you have *actually* sent the email, returned the library book, or paid the bill. Intention has the misleading component of providing a sense of "mental completion" and it is important to follow-up with a reliable way of checking to ensure that intention has become action.

In school, as in life in general, the really big marker events don't happen very often and can be spaced far apart. Morale boosts are often needed *before* the completion of the paper, end of semester, or job acceptance. Therefore try to celebrate small successes and progress that occurs such as finding a relevant article, solving a computer problem, sitting down to *really* write or *really* study, or savoring a compliment from a professor, advisor, or classmate.

Certain tasks and work from each semester can be put in the finished column. Look in a forward direction when you are nearing completion, and try not to be as burdened by "accumulation fatigue" from the load you carried thus far.

> On a daily basis, some progress feels better than no progress, and with continued effort, somehow the work gets done.

MANTRA 8

Productive procrastination is still procrastination

The common urge to procrastinate that finds many students may seem paradoxical: The student feels the powerful forces of wanting to do really well and at the same time experiences opposing forces of wanting to delay or avoid the anxiety-provoking tasks. In order for any avoidance strategy to be viable when you know you "should" be applying yourself, procrastination behaviors can vary and be complex. In applied terms, if something is due or part of the immediate goal equation, then doing something else instead may be considered procrastination. Even productive activity is still procrastination if it takes you away from what is required.

First there are the most obvious forms of student procrastination involving TV or Internet. While you recognize these can be delay tactics, you may rationalize the activity as breaks that take longer than expected. Other procrastination activities may be less obvious because of a beneficial aspect, such as helping others with their academic work concerns while not focusing on your own concerns, putting in additional hours at your job despite increased academic demands, and cleaning your living space beyond what's necessary or usual. While decluttering and cleaning may have a positive effect of increasing one's sense of control and competence, microfocusing on a cleaning task or tackling a nonessential drawer may become a key distraction.

Interconnected forms of procrastination occur when you are doing something related to actual academic work but not moving forward as needed. Examples include: over-researching without any writing, experimenting with organizational systems, refocusing on editing without any important changes, or just working to fine tune a subject that you're already acing and ignoring the work that really needs improvement. Educators see the problem of procrastination with papers frequently and often encourage students to adapt a "write first, edit later" approach. If you picture a simple pie chart, subdivided by tasks that need your attention most and assign how much time has been allotted, you can see how procrastination creates a mismatch of where time is spent versus where time is needed.

Of course the activities listed above can have a helpful place if they are consciously selected in the take-a-break, time-limited category as opposed to any misleading procrastination. Sometimes the most important things are those that you are *not* doing, and the longer you wait, the more difficult it may become — as those who've had the experience of tackling an "incomplete" often attest. Ask yourself: How will this help my studying move forward and be ready for the upcoming test, paper, or presentation? Is it a break or is it ongoing procrastination, albeit productive procrastination? For example, cleaning out your backpack may be a helpful break in service of your academic work, as this can create a sense of order and even remind you of something you may have missed; other tasks may be too major or lead you far off-track. To decrease procrastination anxiety:

- Look at the course material or job application — face it
- Do something about it — act upon it
- Bring in others — seek support for continuing or help for correcting

George Vaillant, M.D., psychiatrist and author of *Adaptations to Life,* has studied healthy adult defense mechanisms for dealing with anxiety, which include: humor — individual definition, universal smiling and laughter benefits; altruism — helping others without seeking reward, can be as simple as holding a door; suppression — being aware of and not forgetting the problem on the list, but putting worry on the back burner to address at the necessary time; sublimation — channeling anxiety into productive work; and anticipation — picturing and preparing for what's next.

Perfectionism is often associated with procrastination, particularly among high-achieving individuals. Perfection, if ever attainable, would certainly be fleeting and unsustainable. If you had a lifetime to write a paper, study for an exam, prepare for a presentation, or research finding a job — it still wouldn't be perfect. Some students who find themselves wrestling with perfectionism may delay embarking upon tasks because it paradoxically removes the pressure for perfection; due to the limits of diminished time, self-expectations for perfection abate, and it reframes the challenge as completing the task by the deadline.

In *Too Perfect: When Being in Control Gets Out of Control,* Allan Mallinger, M.D. and writer Jeannette DeWyze describe perfectionists as hearing a "higher demand" in the task and hence feeling added pressure.

It is important to gain perspective by taking into account the nature of the project and the expectations based on current academic level. Some of the most capable students in all fields may hear this higher demand, particularly in such tasks as completing a thesis or dissertation. Rather than striving towards excellence and meeting degree requirements, a student may be concerned that their research work needs to be perfected to a *monumental* level. Perfectionistic students may not always be aware that their standards can be *beyond* what is expected, and this can have the potential to inhibit productivity. It can be helpful for example, to read recent dissertations that have been accepted in one's department. Seeing completed work has helped many students identify the task as concrete and attainable, and added perspective that fosters dissertation completion. Benchmarking of fair comparisons with other academic standards or employment considerations can provide valuable guidelines for moving forward.

The temptations for productive procrastination will be omnipresent via external stimuli and internal restlessness, which have the possibility to pull attention away from the required task. It takes vigilance and added discipline to stay on topic, avoiding or noting interesting options for a later time.

> This is the time to give your own academic work full attention and effort — productive procrastination can wait after all.

MANTRA 9

Seek clarity for confusion (ASAP)

The academic calendar moves at a fast pace, with each week being an important percentage of time and crunch times never being far away. Spending time being confused may be confounding, as one concept can spill over into the next and snowball to impede or stop progress. At crunch time the need to remedy confusion is more pressing than ever — time is of the essence.

Consulting with a knowledgable source is one of the most efficient ways to get past confusion. Asking questions, seeking clarity, and gaining assistance are basic assertiveness "skills and rights" of effective communication, which are essential, and the topic of many excellent books, university workshops, and mentoring discussions. The most successful students in every field, including lifelong learners and achievers, are the ones who develop proficiency in using the best available resources. Based on the number of offices and services dedicated to student advising, personal and career counseling, and learning and study skills on each campus, it is clear that the university anticipates and strives to address student developmental needs. Obtaining assistance does not diminish independence, but rather adds information and empowers you to meet your goals.

Peers in school and peers in life's every arena are vital for connection, and academic isolation is ill-advised. When confused, it is helpful to compare notes with a classmate about their reaction to the particular assignment or test — you may not be the only one who is struggling, and there may in fact be a broader student issue that is based on an interactive problem with professor, material presentation, or overall classroom comprehension. Classmates can also help sort through questions and help you avoid potential errors in wishful thinking, such as: "Maybe this is not an important topic, Maybe it won't be on the test, and Maybe things will just fall into place."

Professors and Teaching Assistants (T.A.s) often offer review sessions or added office hours during crunch periods. Unfortunately, embarrassment or fear of revealing confusion may get in the way of students asking their questions. I have heard students express these common worries: "How can I ask *now* — it would have been okay if I had asked earlier and looked on top of things. What would the Professor or T.A. think of me — especially someone whom I might ask for a recommendation?" It can be difficult to debate political concerns. Perhaps for students in this situation, it would be helpful to attend the review sessions and write down questions to address later with a non-grading source, such as a private tutor or helpful friend.

If you are truly in trouble with time or addressing the material, it may be necessary to approach the Professor or T.A. for the possibility of receiving additional help, gaining an extension, or obtaining an incomplete or other course of action, such as dropping or withdrawing from the course. While this may be an unfamiliar or uncomfortable position for you to address, keep in mind that professors are versed in handling these student issues. Policy is in place throughout the university to help navigate academic concerns.

Moving quickly at crunch time and being confused are opposing notions that can turn you in circles and make you unproductive. Stopping to acknowledge and assess the confusion will save you time in the long run and yield better results, particularly in consultation with others. It can be difficult to have full perspective when you are in the middle of the situation. Addressing confusion may be more effective as a multi-person effort.

> Asking questions for clarification is a prerequisite to focusing on the essential challenges ahead.

MANTRA 10

Avoid doing something new or risky during crunch time

This mantra is offered in the spirit of prevention and is based on years of witnessing outcomes that can hopefully be avoided or lessened. Crunch time generally has enough pressure and stimulus overload — no need to add any unintended drama to the mix.

During crunch time your energy and brain are taxed to the maximum, and anything that is new requires more attention and alertness than perhaps you can give. Absent-mindedness, preoccupation, and overload stress increase the risk of accidents, mistakes, and losing important items. Murphy's Law of "whatever can go wrong, will" is exponential when pairing novelty and risk at crunch periods, with limited time to correct or recover if something goes wrong.

Below is a list of some key incidents that have occurred with students during crunch time. It is purposefully focused on highlighting seemingly "ordinary" events that may not be given any pre-thought or consideration, as opposed to the usual category of well-known "high risk behaviors."

- Eating somewhere or something you have never eaten before: Students trying a new restaurant or selecting an unknown food item during crunch time may find "X" food or spice not digesting well — or worse, having an allergic reaction that merits a trip to the emergency room.

- Drinking coffee from a different shop or vendor: The amount of caffeine and serving size can make a difference to the caffeine sensitive. It is advisable to walk an extra block, even in the rain, to get your usual coffee order, if you are at risk for an unpredictable reaction.

- Attempting to fix something in your living space that you have never attempted before or do infrequently: Students have reported property holes and leaks, plus personal injuries, especially unfortunate if nothing really needs fixing at that moment (productive procrastination, Mantra 8). For now it might be better to refrain from tackling certain home projects while your brain is preoccupied, leaving such items on the to-do-after-crunch-time list.

- Playing a sport or doing exercises that you have never done previously or do not do routinely: While exercise is a great overall stress reducer, if you are not conditioned for a new activity or underestimate the difficulty of returning to a sport after a long absence the unintended consequence can be soreness or injury. During crunch time, stay with your usual activities or exercise routine or go with the basics of walking.

- Watching an unsettling movie or even viewing a TV episode that features an especially distressing scene: This can have the opposite impact of the intended pleasant diversion or relaxation break, creating agitation or upset instead. Now may be a better time for a more predictable comedy show or other option that will not be distressing or magnify your own concerns. Edit accordingly.

The list goes on, and noteworthy examples also include: helping friends move boxes and furniture that were too heavy to lift comfortably; studying in a different spot, getting distracted, and leaving one's phone somewhere; encountering cleaning mishaps with new products; and getting lost when visiting an unfamiliar location. Misplaced items, damaged belongings, the need for medical attention, and above all, distress and time disruptions are also mentioned.

Certainly, as noted, you need to take breaks—those that you have done before and can predict the outcome as best as possible. Protect yourself with prevention from even seemingly innocuous novelty or unnecessary activities for now. There will be time after the pressing tasks are completed, to think beyond the routine with better attention, energy, and flexibility.

> After all, crunch time is not usual time.

SECTION III
EGO CHALLENGES

In the process of earning an advanced degree, one puts forth ongoing efforts and ideas that are subject to self, peer, and professional review. As in any complex endeavor that is worthwhile, there will be demanding times with potential for both success and setbacks in various academic, career, and social situations.

CAUTION: EGO CHALLENGES AHEAD.

The New York Public Library, as many may know, is an impressive literary institution that is flanked by two marble lion statues, nicknamed "Patience" and "Fortitude." The lions are symbols of what is needed to persevere during challenging times. Summon your own patience and fortitude when tested along the way.

Higher education is a significant developmental process, and at its end, you will be changed from when you first started. Find compassion for uncomfortable stages — you are a work in progress, with an education in progress.

EGO CHALLENGE MANTRAS

- ☐ Try not to rest your ego on one academic measure
- ☐ Educational success goes beyond grades and class rank
- ☐ Academic accidents happen
- ☐ Plan B may be better than Plan A
- ☐ Resumes express accomplishments

MANTRA 11

Try not to rest your ego on one academic measure

Academic achievements are measured by multiple reference points that are gathered sequentially into an overall evaluation process. It may be theoretically possible, but practically impossible, for any student to be equally skilled in requirements and electives, individual and group projects, writing and speaking, research and applied tasks, plus technical and creative abilities — especially, class after class, semester after semester, and beyond.

At any given time you will likely be juggling a variety of assignments or tasks. A challenge to self-esteem can occur when one measure, often to the exclusion of other measures, becomes *the* reference point of significance of your own professional accomplishments or pride. This can range from students "judging" their overall academic ability by an individual performance in a particular course in their major, not getting a certain internship, or whether or not their thesis receives high marks. A self-flagged individual measurement needs to be put into context and examined intently, especially before any conclusions can be made.

As you step back to evaluate the situation and gain perspective, consider the following:

1. How significant is this one measurement, not just to you, but according to the viewpoint of your advisor, professor, or knowledgeable peers? Is this an issue of career consideration that might require correction and readjustment, or is it more a matter of personal disappointment and pride?

2. Why didn't it go as well as you had hoped?

First, there are the self-reflection questions: Did you underestimate the difficulty level or miss some background, didn't put in the necessary hours of work, had difficulty with the professor's instructional style, or experienced a time period rife with personal challenges? Second, consider the external circumstances that were occurring: Was the course skewed to a difficult grading curve, with a smaller number of As allotted in the class? Were you applying for a competitive, oversubscribed internship in which the difference between student you and student other might have been negligible or due to a matter of timing?

Focusing just on one problematic aspect of your academic work or activities, particularly to the exclusion of the total picture, may add stress and the potential for thoughts to skew negatively. In *The Feeling Good Handbook,* psychiatrist David Burns, M.D. outlines "10 Forms of Twisted Thinking" or types of "cognitive distortions" which includes the "mental filter" of "picking out the negative," (the low midterm grade in *this* class is what *really* matters) or "disqualifying the positive" (the other midterms weren't difficult, so *those* successes *don't* count).

Negative thoughts can combine or create a domino effect in worrying beyond the current situation and projecting that one particular incident, which may in fact be containable, will generate other possible sequences of negatives — or "overgeneralization," another example of *twisted thinking.* Negative thoughts need to be monitored, stopped, and addressed by reviewing the full scenario of what has actually happened to date. Aim to make a fair assessment of the situation and identify any needed corrections in concrete terms or thinking paradigm. Bringing focus back to the full picture is essential, because it resumes multiple reference points, and reframing your thoughts helps you to react differently to the same situation.

While you may often be asked certain general questions — where did you go to undergraduate and/or graduate school, what was your major, or what was your research topic — rarely, if ever, will you be asked about individual grades in a subject or specific markers from the past. As others have experienced, you may actually forget an exact measurement over time as it becomes less relevant and eclipsed by new achievements.

> At graduation, your work will be noted in its entirety — in the form of a diploma, conferring a degree with your name.

MANTRA 12

Educational success goes beyond grades or class rank

Many students bring an educational history in which they are accustomed to being at or near the top of their class. This translates into an expectation of finding some grade of "good news" after one's name, knowing the context of one's discipline and school grading standards. Yet sometimes "holding one's own" in a less familiar and very capable group may be the new positive. There is variability in everyone's performance, along with diverse new academic challenges.

Sometimes it is the actual grade in a particular subject that bothers you — you were hoping for an A but got "stung" by a B or introduced to your first C, and so on, and find it hard to get past that letter. The first test grade can be viewed as initial feedback to seek correction as needed. Overall, it is important to acknowledge the context of evaluation within a high achieving group that is studying difficult material and to know when the bar may be set higher. Your grade can be an indication that you are challenging yourself with a difficult course or program and not taking an easy route of a given A; sometimes it's the B in the hardest course that will be seen as an academic triumph.

Grades measure performance, and one may have actually learned more than was exhibited within assessments or tests. Studying to correspond with higher performance outcomes includes thinking, from the very beginning, about the grading measurements vis-à-vis the learning materials, so as to apportion your time and focus where needed. Excellent papers require integration of information and added time for feedback, revisions, and editing. Test-taking strategies include awareness of test format, content focus, and actively thinking of likely questions based on the materials. Preparation can be helped by performing trial runs of realistic test lengths and sample questions in a simulated test environment — sitting upright, no media, no talking, no interruptions. Presentations improve when practiced ahead, in front of an audience who can give feedback and ask questions, and where the factors of content, speaking, and time usage are taken into account. When faced with a stressful task, it is often helpful to be on the side of over-preparedness to address performance challenges, and to strengthen confidence. However if concerns arise about performance being impeded by anxiety, difficulty focusing on instructions or questions, or blanking on answers already known, there are campus professionals or outside referral resources with expertise in the management of test anxiety.

Sometimes the differential involved in obtaining a slightly higher grade in a particular subject may come with much sacrifice of time and energy. If this is necessary for future success, then acknowledge that intent and adapt expectations for intensified effort. For others it may translate into balancing your personal best with awareness of when there may be diminishing rewards for your benefit, especially if it prevents you from accomplishing other work or sacrificing important extra-curricular activities.

Keep in mind that there are varied avenues for students to distinguish themselves within an academic community apart from grade point average or class rank. Here are some of my favorite examples: students who were involved in volunteer and leadership activities receiving special awards at graduation, those in various fields who created start-up businesses, writers for campus newspapers and popular blogs, performers who developed their artistry on various stages, students with interdisciplinary focus engaged in synergistic research and field activities, and others who put added energy into excelling in one particular subject niche. Developmental psychologist Howard Gardner, Ph.D. champions the notion of "multiple intelligences" in which he articulates the following eight categories: linguistic, logic-mathematical, music, spatial, bodily/kinesthetic, interpersonal, intrapersonal, and naturalistic. Names of these "intelligences" have been highlighted by some (such as Daniel Goleman, Ph.D., who helped popularize the term "Emotional Intelligence") and debated by others (*multiple intelligences* versus *multiple abilities*). It is important to note that certain strengths may not be addressed through some common measurements or standardized testing matrixes. Students may be even more successful in clinical practices, leadership positions, and creative endeavors due to their own specific assets.

Across all abilities, achievement will be impacted by one's capacity for "grit." defined as passion plus perseverance. Angela Duckworth, Ph.D., psychology professor and researcher, who extensively studies the topic of grit, reports that grit may be a stronger predictor than intelligence for academic achievements.

Each student needs to embrace their individual talents and interests, as "success" can be defined in many ways and combinations. All abilities have their own importance and are needed contributions to the academic and larger community.

> There are diverse pathways with a multitude of opportunities for you to excel.

MANTRA 13

Academic accidents happen

Any student capable of succeeding in a particular school, program, or activity can also become vulnerable to the confluence of factors producing what I refer to as an "academic accident." This can happen in different combinations and at different intervals, analogous to the way a good driver can have a car accident at some point due to any number of reasons such as poor visibility, slick roads, fatigue, and distraction.

A "perfect academic storm" might occur when a student hits an academic rough patch, becomes sick with

Mantras for Ego Challenges   71

a bad case of the flu, and experiences added stressors, such as a family member's illness or problems with a significant relationship, all occuring in close time proximity. This could tip the dominoes of lost time, lost focus, lost productivity, and lost confidence.

The accident may be minor — cleared up easily by dropping the "extra" class without much consequence, or more major — reworking plans, requiring additional assistance. Like any accident, the first step is to report it to an official source such as the professor, academic advisor, or counseling office in order to assess the problem and possible remedies: drop a class, if within drop/add period; withdraw, if after drop/add period; request an incomplete in the course; apply for a leave of absence in a major circumstance. The more severe the accident, the greater the likelihood of emotional impact and planning issues, with the need for additional assistance to help address the incident.

The "student years" present many developmental challenges due to demographic factors alone, taking place over the span of degree pursuits while interacting with ongoing changes in a complex academic environment. Academic accidents are often linked to the following factors, alone or in combination:

- Undertaking a higher level course for self-challenge, or "placing" too far out of pre-requisites and discovering a gap in foundation knowledge for understanding the range of material to be covered, or struggling in class to keep pace with those with stronger backgrounds.

- Experiencing academic overload by signing up for more than the standard courseload (quantitative overload), or by taking various "heavy" courses that require extra work (qualitative overload), leaving little room for any glitch in a fast-paced, jam-packed calendar.

- Taking a scheduled class with a guest professor who is not known in one's academic community, where class level and demands were not initially well-defined, and accelerated as the semester progressed.

- Opting for a brand new course offering (even with a vetted professor) that does not have a track record, and experiments with requirements and/or difficulty level, which turn out to be an uncertain fit.

- Electing to "stretch" oneself in learning novel information, such as an esoteric field or completely unfamiliar topic, as unrelated and new learning can take more time to gain context and understanding.

- "Transitioning" without noting it as a transition time, such as during expected change considerations in an ongoing program that bring unexpected difficulty. Examples include: enrollment in small seminars that focus on active classroom participation after having taken larger lecture classes only; first set of clinical medical rotations in a demanding area, and independent dissertation or thesis writing following years of structured activities. Such transitions in the middle of programs may not get flagged for support, as opposed to initial entry transitions or final graduation transitions.

- Losing a major advisor, research mentor, or favorite professor who leaves the university or who suffers illness or death, can be a significant loss and readjustment, especially when that relationship played a central role in one's academic life.

- Experiencing personal interference with one's own health or personal life, concerns such as a family member's hospitalization, relationship stress, or financial problem.

- Delaying or refraining from asking for help with academic trouble or personal upset, perhaps because one never needed help before or kept thinking things would resolve with perseverance alone.

There is a common, unified message presented in the academic community which needs to be underscored and amplified: Help is available and help is essential in assisting students to protect and foster academic and personal well-being. Utilize the assistance that is a key part of the educational community for prevention, support, and remedial services.

Academic accidents and near-misses happen more often than the topic gets mentioned, especially when meeting individuals with completed degrees. However, if one were privy to the back-stories of all alumni academic histories, one would learn about various minor and major academic accidents that were experienced and overcome. Sometimes these stories do not surface until the topic is directly relevant, and only then may one hear about others who dropped a class, wrestled with an incomplete, had the experience of taking a leave of absence, or needed to retake a major course, entrance exam, or professional board/licensure.

Psychologists Robert Brooks, Ph.D. and Sam Goldstein, Ph.D. in *The Power of Resilience* noted the importance of "dealing effectively with mistakes" as part of healthy development. Individuals who show resilience do not get easily defeated by mistakes or setbacks but instead seek to learn, grow, and find opportunities as a result. The notion of "failure" or "setbacks" is frequently mentioned in context of those with impressive biographies and is emphasized as a chance for improvement and progress. Think of leaders and innovators across various fields and many popular university commencement speakers. Mistakes are part of the

MANTRA 14

Plan B may be better than Plan A

The assertion that Plan B can turn out to be better than Plan A is not offered as a rationalization but rather as a perspective that is validated with time, over and over again. Initially, it can be an unsettling proposition, whether the switch from Plan A to Plan B is self-initiated or is externally dictated.

Plan A may have been set into motion without having been fully vetted or sustainable for future applications. The circumstances and influence of family human experience, and it is one's response to mistakes that will make the difference in the impact.

> Academic accidents happen. If you find yourself in this situation, engage in self-reflection, gain assistance, and debrief with trusted help before moving on — and then move forward.

and peers, school specialties or institutes, and societal factors can skew towards certain "desirable" choices based on security, popularity, and prestige.

Was Plan A in fact a carefully chosen path for oneself, or more of a default option? Some students may have been initially drawn to the "popular" major, "coveted" job, or "hot" career, only to find it was not the best match for them in one or more key dimensions. The need or preference to alter plans is a common occurrence and can be adapted.

Plan A may be an excellent springboard for exploration and gaining clarity, be it about changing majors, transferring schools, seeking employment elsewhere, or rethinking graduate specialization. Some students realize that the appeal of greater job security was, unfortunately, in an area that did not match their interests. Other students discover that, despite an interesting major and viable work options, they have a stronger preference for attending medical school; conversely, some pre-med students who have previously thought *only* of medical school seek to consider other routes. Many graduate students revise a research topic in order to reflect their changing career interests; others add a completely new degree focus to an existing work history. Career "pangs" that persist over time can be hard to ignore, even when they are inconvenient to address.

A key task in positive career development is finding the "best home" for the idea. This entails separating out and repositioning varied positive components and understanding why certain other parts do not fit well, including environmental or timing factors.

Sometimes Plan A may be not seem "right," yet it is difficult to articulate another plan instead. Most campuses have professionals and various offices designated to career counseling and testing, planning, and advising. Helpful career exploration also includes reading relevant material, interviewing others in the field, preferably at different stages and practice situations, and job shadowing to see the real life translation. It is important to speak with professionals and students who feel positively about their work and to also understand specific drawbacks. For example, 50% travel could be a benefit or a spoiler in different cases. It can be especially helpful to find someone whose career life resembles that which you'd like to embrace, as the presence of role models can be important in clarifying and reaching goals.

The interdisciplinary focus in many fields and universities may in fact encourage a hybrid of plans, including double majors and dual degree programs within and across schools. One favorite suggestion is to survey the campus bookstore's section of required reading texts for current course offerings to gain an overview of career options, combinations, and possible matches with one's own interests. Plan B may ultimately yield a similar outcome to Plan A, while taking a different route. For example, students may be advised to enter a master's program to strengthen their record for doctoral admission or to obtain particular work experience. There is an added dimension of adjustment when Plan B is not one's original intent or preference. Plan B may enroll you in a business, graduate, or law school or clinical assignment that was not your first choice, bringing up disappointment to say the least.

However, in time, the same students may reflect back with satisfaction, and often real surprise, upon the unexpected set of opportunities and exposure to particular academic, employment, or social realms, which perhaps would not have occurred otherwise. Positive outcomes include meeting an influential mentor for career development, discovering a specialty interest offered in that particular institution, enjoying a different geographic location, or finding a relationship or meeting new friends whom one might never have encountered.

It is also important to note that sometimes Plan B may turn out to be transitional and useful as a bridge to create other opportunities. By doing excellent work, some students have utilized Plan B as a stepping stone to academic transfers, relocations, or redirections after a certain time period when it seemed more fitting to move forward.

Plan Bs may also require additional time and effort, including taking more courses and meeting field requirements. Some will need to return to school for intensive refocus such as the "post-bac" programs for medical, veterinary, or dental school entrance or nursing requirements. Such plan Bs are not automatic, and they require strong commitment to meet the strenuous demands. Worthwhile endeavors are often difficult to obtain and can be expected to present higher entry barriers. Randy Pausch, Ph.D., the computer science professor at Carnegie Mellon memorialized by his *Last Lecture,* talked powerfully about "brick walls" being there not to block us out, but as an opportunity to challenge us to prove how much we want to attain the goal.

Keep your key strengths in mind when assessing the challenges of career options and investigating new fields. Martin Seligman, Ph.D., psychology professor and researcher, in his book entitled *Flourish,* emphasizes the role of "signature strengths," defined as an individual's self-rated top attributes that are central to their being, such as "love of learning." Utilizing your signature strengths can inform meaningful decision-making and promote overall well-being and happiness.

Higher education may present a lifetime of anticipated and unanticipated opportunities, and possible changes in career aspects. One may be interested in fields that are in the beginning stages of development, or moving to specialties that might not even exist at this moment in time.

Periodically evaluate your interests and opportunities in order to recommit, revise, or create new plans.

MANTRA 15

Resumes express accomplishments

Most students will need a revised resume or curriculum vitae ("CV" for academic or research positions) that focuses on education, work experience, and academic accomplishments in the best possible context; it is meant to be positive. However, resumes or CVs may stir up mixed emotions, especially when linked with uncertainty involved in completing applications for the next academic program, internship, or job.

Certain questions typically ensue in social conversations that may encroach on "sensitive" topics: "How's the job search, internship, graduate school, dissertation, or 'relationship' progressing?" Sometimes the question is more pointed such as "When will you be finished with your thesis?" or "What will you do next?" Your reactions can vary based on your changing circumstances and interactions. Some prepare a "social answer" of the "coming along" or "time will tell" genre, which is a type of "fog" that acknowledges the question without giving any real information. Others deftly change the topic and pivot attention to a different focus. Assertiveness is an important life skill in managing stress. As psychologists Robert Alberti, Ph.D. and Michael Emmons, Ph.D. describe in *Your Perfect Right,* you don't need to respond with more than is "comfortable." There is a choice involved in self-disclosure. If you deem it to be helpful, purposefully address your current situation more fully at the time and/or opt to seek out others to gain assistance, networking, or moral support.

Resumes may be difficult to write or edit completely by oneself (campus career services and others can help). Some students report not liking the task of translating their lives into resume format. Self-promotion is not automatic for many accomplished individuals who may underestimate experiences that others might view as impressive, including unique items such as "internal awards" from prior organizations.

In my practice, I find it meaningful, especially for those making transitions, to also create an "annotated" resume, separate from the "public" version, articulating with candor details about one's activities, environment, and personal reactions. This exercise can reveal that a person may consider one job great because of the people, while another job, although prestigious and in a great location, translates as quite miserable because of its monotonous focus on details. Factors of preference and personal style, including extraversion and introversion dimensions, may impact your feelings and thoughts about a particular work environment or job duties. The emphasis upon career matching and personal style, based on *Myers-Briggs Type Indicator,* is expressed in detail within Paul D. Tieger and Barbara Barron-Tieger's book *Do What You Are.*

It is also helpful to recount extracurricular focus, hobbies, and leisure activities that may or may not make it onto the resume but can provide useful information for customizing a plan of work activities that complement avocationally what you are doing for your job or studies. Often it's important to look back in time, if certain of your valued activities were shelved due to increased academic commitments or difficulty in finding outlets. In the process, you may note other activities that you have *not* explored to date, but which still hold interest, such as taking a photography course or learning a new language.

While the resume recounts the past, it also provides important perspective on future planning. It helps you to imagine placeholders for subsequent accomplishments and provides updates of what you might want to continue, change, or expand for your career portfolio and goals.

Success can happen at various points in a career and is not a linear process. Writer Brendan Gill, who logged many years of experience as a contributor to *The New Yorker,* profiled in his book *Late Bloomers* individuals from diverse fields whose greatest achievement *occurred* or was *recognized* in mid-life and beyond. Ultimately, it will be your own definition of success that really matters. Many successful professionals with external validation and awards feel something is missing if they have not yet achieved a *specific* accomplishment that is important to themselves, such as addressing a particular research problem, writing a children's book, or working in another country.

This career "bucket list," or one's own agenda, is important to keep in mind in the midst of life's ongoing noise and busyness. Identifying learning goals and meeting new learning challenges will help maintain cognitive fitness, relevancy, and personal satisfaction in years to come. Continue to update and strengthen your perspective and your strategies with accompanying supports, including your own Academic Mantras, for the achievement of future goals. Throughout any subsequent resume additions and revisions, your education will always be represented as a permanent and significant accomplishment, which becomes an enduring part of your professional history.

> The degree-seeking phase of education may be finite, but learning is for a lifetime!

Index

academic transitions, 1, 11-14, 72-73, 79-80
Alberti, Robert, 83
assertiveness, 50-51, 82-83
Bloch, Arthur, 5
Branden, Nathaniel, 19-20
Bridges, William, 1
Bronfenbrenner, Urie, 1
Brooks, Robert, 74
Burns, David, 63
Clance, Pauline, 27
DeWyze, Jeannette, 47
Duckworth, Angela, 68
Dweck, Carol, 23
Emmons, Michael, 83
Folkman, Susan, 14
Gardner, Howard, 68
Gill, Brendan, 85
Goldstein, Sam, 74
Goleman, Daniel, 68
grit, 68-69
Hassles and Uplifts Scale, 14
healthy defense mechanisms, 47
Holmes and Rahe Stress Scale, 7-8
homesickness, 10-11
hurried sickness, 31
Imes, Suzanne, 27
Impostor phenomenon (IP Scale), 27-28
intention, 43
Kabat-Zinn, Jon, 31
Lazarus, Richard, 14
life event change, 7-11
Mallinger, Allan, 47
Maslow, Abraham, and Hierarchy of Needs, 33
Medina, John, 34
mindset, fixed and growth, 23
multiple intelligences, 68
Murphy's Law, 5, 41, 55
Myers-Briggs Type Indicator, 84
Neugarten, Bernice, 10
Pareto Principle, 41
Parkinson's Law, 40-41
Pausch, Randy, 80
perfectionism, 47-48

performance/learning,
  groundwork, 13-15, 22, 24
  operationalizing, 39-40,
  66-67
procratination alerts, 45-49
reframing,
  cognitive distortions, 63-64,
  perfectionism, 47-48
  setbacks, 74-75, 79
resilience, 74-75, 79-80
Rosen, Larry, 42
self awareness, 4, 9, 28-29,
  34-35, 42, 71-73
self-care, 34-36
self-esteem, 18-20, 29-30
Seligman, Martin, 80
Selye, Hans, 37
signature strengths, 80
Simon, Herbert, 24
social clock, 10, 12
stress management,
  adaptation cycle, 37
  eustress/distress, 8
  fight or flight, 42
  outlets, 14, 35-36, 46, 57
Thayer, Robert, 36
Tieger, Paul and Barbara, 84
time management,
  fixed/variable, 41-42
  key time rules, 40-42
  quantitative/qualitative overload, 72

utilizing resources,
  career, 28, 78-79, 83-84
  consultation for information/perspective, 14, 39, 50-52
  resolving academic concerns, 52, 71, 73-75
Vaillant, George, 47

Suggested readings

Alberti, Robert E. and Michael L. Emmons. *Your Perfect Right: Assertiveness and Equality in Your Life and Relationships,* 9th ed. Atascadero, CA: Impact Publishers, 2008.

Bloch, Arthur. *Complete Book of Murphy's Law: A Definitive Collection.* Los Angeles: Price Stern Sloan, Inc., 1991.

Branden, Nathaniel. *The Six Pillars of Self-Esteem.* New York: Bantam, 1994.

Bridges, William. *Transitions: Making Sense of Life's Changes,* 2nd ed. Cambridge, MA: De Capo Press, 2004.

Brooks, Robert and Sam Goldstein. *The Power of Resilience: Achieving Balance, Confidence and Personal Strength in Your Life.* New York: McGraw-Hill, 2004.

Burns, David. D. *Feeling Good: The New Mood Therapy.* New York: Avon, 1980, 1999.

Charlesworth, Edward A. and Ronald G. Nathan. *Stress Management: A Comprehensive Guide to Wellness.* New York: Atheneum, 1984.

Suggested Readings

Clance, Pauline Rose. *The Impostor Phenomenon: Overcoming The Fear That Haunts Your Success.* Atlanta: Peachtree Publisher, LTD 1985.

Dweck, Carol S. *Mindset: The New Psychology of Success.* New York: Ballantine, 2006.

Gardner, Howard. *Multiple Intelligences: New Horizons in Thinking.* New York: Basic Books, 2006.

Goleman, Daniel. *Emotional Intelligence: Why It Can Matter More than IQ.* New York: Bantam, 1995.

Gill, Brendan. *Late Bloomers: 75 Remarkable People Who Found FAME, SUCCESS, & JOY in the Second Half of Their Lives.* New York: Artisan, 1996.

Kabat-Zinn, Jon. *Arriving At Your Own Door: 108 Lessons in Mindfulness.* New York: Hyperion, 2007.

Knaus, William. *Do It Now!: Break the Procrastination Habit.* New York: John Wiley & Sons, 1979, 1998.

Mallinger, Allan E. with Jeannette De Wyze. *Too Perfect: When Being in Control Gets Out of Control.* New York: Clarkson Potter/Publishers, 1992.

Medina, John. *Brain Rules: 12 Principles for Surviving and Thriving at Work, Home, and School.* Seattle: Pear Press, 2008.

Pausch, Randy with Jeffrey Zaslow. *The Last Lecture.* New York: Hyperion, 2008.

Rosen, Larry. *iDisorder: Understanding Our Obsessions With Technology and Overcoming Its Hold On Us.* New York: Palgrave Macmillan, 2012.

Seligman, Martin. *Flourish*. New York: Free Press, 2011.

Thayer, Robert. *Calm Energy: How People Regulate Mood with Food and Exercise*. New York: Oxford University Press, 2001.

Tieger, Paul D. and Barbara Barron-Tieger. *Do What You Are: Discover The Perfect Career For Your Through The Secrets of Personality Type*. Boston: Little, Brown and Company, 1995.

Vailliant, George. *Adaptations to Life*, 2nd ed. Cambridge, MA: Harvard University Press, 1998.